MW01485414

Beyond the Breakwall

A LAKE ERIE SAILOR'S BOOK OF POETRY AND MUSINGS

Kyle B. Smith

Dedicated to the new generation of sailors

Preface

Ironically, this preface is being written after numerous edits and modifications of the rest of the book; and I have found it the most difficult.

Initially, I am astounded that I have been sailing on Lake Erie for thirty years. It's an overused cliché, but I don't know where the time has gone. I'm more surprised that I am writing a book of poetry about sailing on Lake Erie after growing up in Southern California, hating my high school English classes, and becoming violently seasick every time I sailed on the Pacific.

But I've learned a lot about myself and my place in the world during the last thirty years while sailing on Lake Erie. I've learned the lessons of sail:

1. Slow can be very good. There's no better way to experience all that the Lake can offer than by sailing on it at five knots, or anchored in a quiet bay. While sailing, we have time to absorb all that is going on around us, and we are better for it. There is no need for speed.
2. Journeys bring enlightenment, and are often more important than destinations.
3. Pay attention to the little things. A loose 25 cent hose clamp can sink you.
4. Take care of your boat and your boat will take care of you.

Perhaps most importantly, I have learned that Lake Erie, despite our failings and abuse, remains truly a Great Lake and worthy of our love and protection.

Whatever I have learned has come from the great friends with whom I have sailed during this past thirty years, and it is to these Lake Erie sailors from Ashtabula, Port Stanley, Erie and Port Dover that I dedicate this book of poetry. A few people deserve a very special thanks:

To my wife Lorraine, who through 26 years of marriage has steadfastly supported my addiction to sail and shared many a summer cruise when I know she would rather be on a golf course.

To Jim, who taught me to sail, and who has exhibited extra-ordinary patience in teaching me zen and the fine art of sailboat maintenance, and the significance of .005 inch. And to his wife Carrie, with whom I shared the high side rail during many a cold and wet race in the early years.

To Terry and Jeanne, and Art and Bonnie, who have provided much inspiration and encouragement for my poetry and this collection.

To Carl Anderson, Nevin Hoefert and the other sailors of AYC who helped me become a better sailor, and shamed me and others into racing on wet, cold and windy days when common sense and self preservation dictated instead bagels and a Bloody Mary in a warm and dry cabin on board Tamara (at the dock!)

To Heather and Murray, Don Wilson and the sailors in Port Stanley who have cruised the Caribbean for years after retiring at a reasonable age and shown me who really did win the War of 1812. Some of these sailors have taught me that, with a little bit of luck, you can sail almost anything across Lake Erie and survive it.

To Ash and Mary, Doug and Diane and the sailors at Port Dover, Ontario, both at PDYC and the Outer Harbour for their friendship, dinners at dock and home, and really great corn.

To Gary and Kay Fritts, Bill H, and Neala, Ian and Christian for introducing me to racing at EYC and the Interclub in 2012.

A special thanks to Mike Adley, Gary Fritts, Terry Persily, Don Stark, Brad Arnold, Joe Scott and unknown others for providing and sharing some great photographs, which really help make this book.

Lastly, and most importantly, a special thanks to Steven Gibbens, a promising young graphic designer, who worked tirelessly, and put up with many edit changes, to produce this book and, without whom, this book would have remained lost on my C drive.

Kyle B. Smith
Caol ila Gael
Ashtabula, Ohio

Table of Contents

I. INTRODUCTION

II. KETTLE CREEK POETRY

III. SAILING ON A GREAT LAKE

IV. PEOPLE POETRY

V. THE CONNECTION

Introduction

This is a collection of poetry I've written over the last twenty years about sailing on Lake Erie. I began writing the poems in a small pub in Port Stanley, Ontario, after an annual sailboat race from Ashtabula, Ohio, across the Lake to Port Stanley, The Lake Erie International Race, (LEIR) involves two sailing clubs, the Port Stanley Sailing Squadron and the Ashtabula Yacht Club. The race is a tradition of legendary beginnings. Nobody knows for sure when it started or why the race began between these two Lake Erie ports. For most of us, LEIR has always been there and we continue the tradition of crossing the Lake, much like migratory birds. The original sailors who began the race have since passed, but the old-timers among us guess that the race may be approaching its 50th anniversary.

Likewise, the origins of the poetry are also a little foggy. At one point about twenty years ago, I wrote and read my first poem after just such a crossing, and after more than a few pints of Smithwicks Irish Ale at a quaint and friendly pub at the Kettle Creek Inn. Each year the poetry just kept coming, reaching a collection of more than twenty poems. The noon poetry reading at the Kettle Creek Inn has thus become a tradition as well.

Traditions seem to be an essential fabric in human existence, linking individuals to a larger group. My poetry is grounded on several traditions: that of sailing boats on wind power alone as we humans have done for thousands of years; an international race between Americans and Canadians that has lasted for almost 50 years; and a friendly gathering of sailors after the race at the Kettle Creek Inn to drink hearty ale and enjoy each other's company after crossing a Great Lake, sometimes under harrowing conditions. It is altogether fitting that following the noon reading, our rabbi Jeff leads us in the Hava Nagila, "come let us rejoice!" We have made yet another crossing.

I didn't realize how much the lake could offer, however, until my wife and I began to cruise Lake Erie for three weeks every August on our 36 foot C&C sailboat, *Caol Ila Gael*. When I am on the lake, I am always stunned by the vast amount of fresh water surrounding me; by its cleanliness and clarity. I am relaxed by the gentle sound of the bow wake as the boat glides easily through the water, and I am rejuvenated by the freshness of the air. Amazingly, twenty five miles out, out of sight of land, sparrows, butterflies and flies appear from nowhere to alight on the boat deck for the long ride to shore. The Lake offers broad sandy beaches, protected bays and a never ending parade of eagles, cormorants, seagulls and other birds depedent on this Great Lake habitat. Sunsets and starlit nights create life long memories.

These experiences, and generous amounts of Chardonnay or Smithwicks, led to more poetry which comprises the second part of this collection as I developed a better awareness and appreciation of sailing boats, the Lake, and the people who sail upon her waters. I discovered the deep currents connecting the Lake, the people who sail upon her waters, and the wood and fiberglass boats with whom we share our identity.

But the foundation remains the Lake itself: one of five fresh water Great Lakes formed more than 10,000 years ago from retreating glaciers. A massive reservoir of fresh water found nowhere else on the planet and perhaps even the universe. The Lake is simply incredible. It never ceases to amaze, to create wonder or surprise. There is much more to Lake Erie than first meets the eye.

The Lake has quiet beginnings. Its main tributary, the Detroit River, flows quietly into the Lake through flatlands and islands just north of Toledo in the far end of the western basin. The western basin is shallow, and even sailboats coming down the Detroit River into the Lake must stay in the shipping channel for more than five miles into the Lake to the Detroit River Light, to avoid groundings before tacking east.

There are other tributaries of muddy, slow moving rivers that flow into the Lake further east: the Maumee, Sandusky, Cuyahoga, Grand and Ashtabula rivers, and numerous creeks on both sides of the Lake.

Fortunately, the Lake is big. The Lake extends more than 250 miles east across one Canadian province and four states, and is more than 60 miles wide at its widest point. The Lake is so big, it creates its own weather patterns with summer off-shore breezes and winter lake effect snows that can bury the shoreline from Cleveland to Buffalo under three feet of snow.

The Lake is also wonderfully diverse. In the middle is wide open water. But to the west are the beautiful islands of Kellys, South Bass, Middle Bass and Pelee which attract millions of tourists each year. The islands are also the site of Commodore Perry's naval victory over the British fleet that secured Lake Erie for the United States during the war of 1812. Kellys Island still shows the grooves carved from solid rock during the last glacial period 10,000 years ago. Pelee Island is a wildlife preserve and well known bird sanctuary.

Further east the Lake gets deeper, the shoreline higher and the water clearer. The shoreline can be rocky or marked by broad beaches bringing throngs of people on hot summer days. Many such beaches at Euclid, Geneva on the Lake, Port Dover and Port Stanley built great dance halls during the 30's and 40's on the beach and sometimes over the water that brought the biggest names in entertainment. My dad remembers Tommy Dorsey, Glen Miller and the other greats passing regularly through Geneva on the Lake. Cedar Point, near Sandusky, has one of the best amusement parks in the world.

Moving east are two great sandy tree–covered peninsulas at Presque Isle and Long Point. Long Point Bay, on the north shore of the Lake, is a haven for some of the best fishing on Lake Erie, if not the world. Presque Isle, on the south shore, almost fully encloses Erie Bay except for a narrow channel for shipping traffic, and is famous because Commodore Perry built his Lake Erie fleet in its protected waters. Both are protected preserves for migrating birds, and they both have great beaches.

There are industrial, commercial and fishing ports on both sides of the Lake. They share in common breakwalls built of rock and sometime concrete that extend into the Lake to accommodate the big freighters that haul coal and iron ore throughout the Great Lakes and the world. Breakwalls are important features in Lake Erie, not only protecting harbors for commercial shipping but also providing shelter for marinas and clubs for recreational boating. The breakwalls were built for the big boats, but the little boats have found a home behind them as well.

Breakwalls provide an important security blanket. Beyond the breakwall, however, is the Lake: clean water, fresh air and a lifetime of adventure and destinations to tempt and tease sailboats and sailors to leave the comforts and protections of docks and harbors.

I have learned, as many have, that the Lake is not a passive receptacle where water comes in and goes out like some kind of giant bathtub. The Lake is wild, and those that enter it do so not on their terms but on those of a Lake that has been around for 10,000 years and always had its way. Lake Erie weather is notoriously unpredictable; sometimes, despite the weather forecast, the winds can build and the water can become turbulent challenging both boat and sailor.

But there is magic in the Lake. Muddy river water may flow quietly into the Lake from various sources, but it does not leave the same. Traveling east, the Lake transforms, clarifies and energizes the Water until, near Buffalo, the Lake water has changed dramatically. The Lake channels its water into one deep, clean and swift moving current into the Niagara River, building such energy and force as to cut deep into solid rock as millions of gallons of Lake water cascade hundreds of feet down the Niagara Escarpment. The wonder of Niagara Falls is created by Lake Erie.

Importantly, the Lake transforms not only its water but anyone who seeks it. After sailing Lake Erie, nobody remains the same. After sailing on the Lake for almost thirty years, my thinking is clearer and my passions run deeper, swifter and more true. I like to think that this poetry is a reflection of my journey of self discovery, and also a reminder that the journey starts beyond the breakwall.

LAKE ERIE: NO HOG BUTCHER OF THE WORLD

With apologies to Chicago and Carl Sandburg, or at least Carl Sandburg

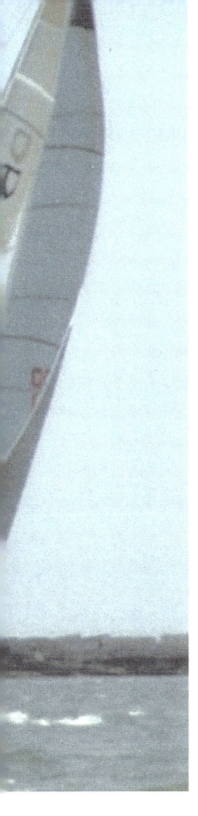

Lake Erie
No hog butcher of the world
Nor freight handlers or toolmakers
Or player of railroads
Nor fodder for jokes on late night TV

Rather faunt of holy water
Borne from ancient virgin glaciers
Giver of Life to millions
Plants, fish, bird and mammal
All receiving communion
from the same overflowing Cup of Life

Lake Erie
Cupped hand of history
Scars of its violent birth
Deep grooves carved into solid rock
Battleground of senseless wars
Not of its choosing
Route to freedom for those whom we enslaved
Denied their own humanity
Shimmering Light for immigrants
For hope
For those who built with their sweat and their blood
The most powerful industrial complex in the world

Lake Erie
Creator of character
People burdened who endure
Lake effect snows, cold and ice
Recession followed by recession
And piles of growing rust and waste
And home of the Cleveland Browns

But the Lake transubstantiates
And redeems and cleanses
Dirty brown river water from many sources
Rushing into a river of clear deep water
Powering mighty turbines, energizing cities
Tumbling and falling hundred of feet into a gorge
It cut by itself from solid rock
Reminding us all that
Whatever Lake Erie takes in
Comes out better.

Beyond the Breakwall

Sometimes, when I raise my sails for open waters
There's a moment when I hesitate and courage falters
As land disappears and I am alone in the sea
I sense the vastness and waves of uncertainty

There is no sense in looking for a guarantee
When you sail outside the harbor of security
Spread your wings and become once again free
Become one with the wind and this freshwater sea

The sails quickly fill and the breeze blows fair
spray and my spirits fly high in the air
She is a solid boat and she does her job well
Slicing through waves and casting her spell.
Happily rising to meet the oncoming swell

The Lake is free and you chart your own course
The wind and the compass your only resource
No roads or signs to dictate direction
Choices without hindsight or time for reflection
live with what happens, for better or worse.

Sails Unfurled

Taking time to find myself
Leaving a safe harbor for open seas
My sails are unfurled

Kettle Creek Poetry

My first and best source of inspiration has been, and will always be, the annual sailboat race between Ashtabula and Port Stanley called the Lake Erie International, a race that can draw up to fifty boats per year. It is a wonderful tradition whose beginnings, like most good traditions, are shrouded in the mists of time, stale beer and aging memories.

The LEIR is sponsored by both the Ashtabula Yacht Club and the Port Stanley Sailing Squadron, separated by 48 miles across the Lake. Port Stanley, Ontario was named after Baron George Stanley, whose son Frederick Stanley became Governour General of Canada, and for whom was named hockey's Stanley Cup. It is a wonderful coastal community with live theatre, arts, beaches and great bars and restaurants and, most importantly, the Kettle Creek Inn.

Ashtabula is a larger city that is slowly working its way out of an industrial recession that has plagued many communities. There is no better example of Ashtabula's Renaissance than the Ashtabula Harbor where derelict buildings have given way to great restaurants, coffee shops, and tempting retail stores. Ashtabula has been a historic harbor for almost 200 years. Ashtabula was built in the Harbor and its future remains in the Harbor.

Ashtabula and Port Stanley have a long history of shipping and commerce that predates the sailboat race, dating back to the days before the American Civil War. The commerce has long since died, but the sailboat racing is brisk and competitive, and the friendships very strong.

A small group of AYC sailors discovered the Kettle Creek Inn, in downtown Port Stanley after an LEIR race in the late 1980's or so. The Inn has maybe 30 rooms, a fine Canadian restaurant, and a folksy pub with wooden floors. The place is owned and operated by Jean, an ex-husband and two sons and is a destination point by itself. Jean always carries a fresh keg of Smithwick Irish ale and serves it properly in traditional British pint glasses.

The LEIR occurs over the July 1-4 weekend, commemorating both Canadian and American holidays of Independence. Depending on how the holiday falls, AYC may sail to Port Stanley and race back to Ashtabula, or PSSS may sail to Ashtabula and race back to Port Stanley. Either way, with a little planning, most of us have a layover day in Port Stanley either before or after the race.

For twenty years we have faithfully gathered at the pub on the layover day for the noon reading (at high noon or whenever we damn well feel like it). More recently, others have joined in the traditional poetry reading, including Ed, a fine Irish tenor, Allan, a great opera voice, and Jeff, our "rabbi" (Imagine, if you can, Henny Youngman without the violin).

The recurring theme of this event is tradition, for which there are many: the race itself, the gathering at a great pub and the art of sailing. These are traditions that would please the old sailors.

I'm not sure why these traditions are so important. Maybe its sheer boredom and people are simply trying to fill up some empty time. But I suspect that its more than that; perhaps a tribal like ritual helps cement the relationships between those who cross the lake by wind power, reaffirming our own identity and those of close friends. Truthfully, I am closer to this group of sailors than almost anyone else in my life. Regardless of weather or forecasts, we cross the Lake together and we make it together. By our traditions, we celebrate the core of life itself—our connection to our world and the people we share it with, something I suspect our species has done for thousands of years in more "primitive" settings.

We celebrate a safe and successful passage across the Lake. Safe passage across forty-eight miles of open water, even in our modern era, can be dangerous if taken for granted. Sometimes boats breakdown. I have seen at least two boats lose propeller blades or transmission couplings. One boat lost a spreader and couldn't tack (fortunately, only one tack was needed), and the crew of another boat spent hours bailing water coming in through the cabin floor. A good friend, and an experienced sailor (he won the race three times) missed Port Stanley by ten miles to the west one year, when he placed his new stereo speakers too close to his compass.

Sometimes the crossings are difficult with punishing winds and high waves. Sometimes there is no wind at all and boats drift in circles on a glassy Lake, sails flapping, under a hot summer sun and biting black flies. Sometimes we dodge or try to outrun thunderstorms—truly a religious experience when your sixty foot aluminum mast is the highest point for 25 miles around. And then sometimes an unexpected squall line knocks the boat down.

But we survive it all and ritualize the passage, we celebrate because we did it together, regardless of the crossing, the only condition necessary is that we shared the experience together.

The Kettle Creek Inn is a very special place for us, and important to the tradition. It is hallowed ground, a sort of Stonehenge where sailors gather near the summer solstice to celebrate a Lake, a crossing and each other. At night, cool breezes flow through the pub and the candle light flickers. If you listen carefully, (and if you've had enough to drink), you can hear the voices of the old sailors of the Lake lifting a glass of highland whiskey to those who have followed in their wakes.

And a special thanks to Jean, a lovely lady and dear friend who runs a very classy and sophisticated Canadian Inn for all but one day of the year, when she permits a group of somewhat unruly sailors to overrun her pub for a few hours, drink a few ales, share friendship and stories, sing and dance, and read poetry. The old sailors would approve.

Ode to Port Stanley

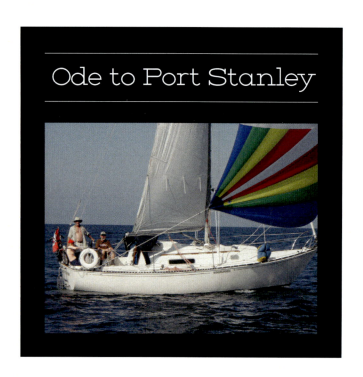

Faraway places and sailboat races
Bright painted hulls and warm smiling faces
Two rivers converge we embrace at its mouth
Where one flows from the north and one from the south

We are among friends who worship the winds
And toast to each other with rare Scottish blends
As Art settles in with his tongue in cheek grin
Downing ales and tall tales at the Kettle Creek Inn

Music at Walter's and fries on the beach
Are almost as good as a Tartan beam reach
I ponder the lessons that Art patiently teaches
Slacken your halyards and loosen your leaches

But the feelings are pure and our friendships endure
And we look forward again to the next trans lake tour
Despite clumsy lift bridges that never raise soon
Silly poetry readings at Saturday noon
Currency exchanges and the two dollar loon
And I-68's and their government goons.

Ode to Bonnie B

Art Benson was a great friend, and an incredible and unforgettable character at the Ashtabula Yacht Club. He was smart and a very good sailor who could fix or jury-rig anything, and the creator of many "artie-isms", my favorite being "fix it until its broke." Every sail with Art was an adventure as hinted in this next poem which is in fact a tribute to his wife.

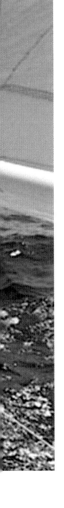

She's kind hearted and sort of a softie
Quick with a smile and hot cup of coffee
A bottle of vodka she's been known to carry
And from thin air she can produce a great bloody mary
She encourages quietly without uttering a word
And she no longer wonders why the engine cannot be heard

An evening sail to the middle of the lake
Can we guess what Artie forgot to take
The wind is light, the boat slow as a mule
The engine won't start, honey, were plumb out of fuel

Or motoring into 30 knot winds
Can we guess what Artie forgot to tend
The anchor is stuck and the freighter can't pass
Don't worry honey, we're just out of gas

He's a good hearted bloke
who avoids a repair until he's sure that its broke
He looks for that drink that will settle his estate
Then lights up a cigarette and leaves it to fate

After a hard night at the Kettle Creek Inn
And a trip to the wine bar that made his head spin
He stumbled and crawled home with a satisfied grin
tripping over his lifelines and headfirst falling in
She peeks over the pillow and into his eyes
There's honesty and candor without a disguise
She knows what he's done and to where he has been
And she lifts up the covers and lets him crawl in.

Ode to the Canadians

Waters we share that bring us together
Despite winds zero to ten and inclement weather
Through bloodthirsty flies and gnats in our eyes
Nothing can separate us, come hell or highwater

Americans and Canadians, what the hell is the difference
History or legends we can make our own inference
We call Lake Erie our home and we treat it with care
Prostrate and praying to the gods of sun and good air

You use kilos but pounds is our weigh
We say hello and you reply "eh"
Our money looks bland and you speak with an accent
Silly differences we maximize beyond meaningful extent
You joke about politics but you have no room to crow
Yes we have Bill Clinton and you had Trudeau

So we meet once again at the Kettle Creek Inn
We're here altogether so let the drinking begin
Enjoying the company of good friends and stout crew
Lift high our glasses and pledge friendships to renew
To our friends one and all, this Smithwicks for you

Swallows to Capistrano

Once every three years or more, we race to Ashtabula from Port Stanley. We always try to work in a night sail from Ashtabula.

Night sails are spectacular. We leave the dock at sunset to the tunes of Dave Brubeck and before long it is dark with billions of stars above. The air is cool and the conversations easy and varied, and the boat sails smoothly on the evenings "off shore" breeze. We watch carefully for other boats, particularly freighters but distances can be deceiving and when we come to close, a freighter will let out five blasts or shine a lights on our sails.

Sometimes we go below for a nap, with the sounds of Lake Erie water swishing less than an inch of fiberglass beyond our heads. About 3 am someone brings out a cold bucket of KFC and a cold beer to wash it down. Dawn comes and we are generally a few miles off Port Stanley.

These sails are great sails and great memories, and there is no one better to sail with than Thad, Dan, Bruce, Big John and "Sam".

With a waddle and a dawdle we load our boat with beer
And food and other junk that almost sank us at the pier
A quick dash for the GPS and a set of moldy charts
The drinking is underway before from 'Bula we depart

We clear the lighthouse as the sun begins to set
By then we are well hoisted and the sails are somewhat set
Thad is on the tiller and Danny at the mast
We've only left the harbor but we're more than halfway gassed

We motored in the night much against our druthers
The engine burned and prop blades turned, for us better than for others
But the breeze picked up as the moon slid west
We sailed a reach which the Spot loves best

We flew north dancing over the waves
Who needs fan belts, impellers and propeller blades
Surfing down waves making more than seven knots
Tell me again what powerboats have that we ain't got.

We dodge a freighter there and a drilling platform here
For we are intrepid sailors without the common sense of fear
We see land shadows to the north as the early dawn appears
Our timing is impeccable for we're almost out of beers

So we have returned, like the buzzards to Hinckley
But reeking of stale beer and bodyparts quite stinkley
We have followed our friends the Canada geese
To this hallowed haven of friendship and of peace

Like the swallows to Capistrano it's magic we gather here
At the same wooden tables and with the same pints of beer
At this same hour of the day and on this same month of the year
Let us toast to each other, til we fall on our rears.

Kettle Creek Speaks

Each May from bursting flowers spring
Soft summer breezes that will dance and sing
Upon the waters in a few impatient weeks
And their song the Kettle Creek to us will speak

It's not about the Inn or Walter's that exude such charm
Nor the artists, the bars and tobacco farms
Certainly not the Outer Harbor which smells and reeks
That is not the Kettle Creek that in May will speak

Kettle Creek is not of places but friendly faces
Of friends who share our lives and sailing races
Our paths may part but this weekend we are seeking
Our friendship, and this is what the Kettle Creek is speaking

Of friendship that exceeds the years
Beyond the boats and many beers
At sunset a single malt to tweak
And this is what the Kettle Creek in May will speak

I've ended many a verse for better or worse
To toast each other with Smithwicks of course
But now put down your beer—for the moment nada
To see who can remember the words to "Oh Canada" *

* *Some Canadians I know claim not to remember the words to their national anthem, at least until they have a few beers. For Americans, it is worth remembering that Canada is a sovereign nation that celebrates an incredible cultural diversity, a strong economy and proud history (which won independence and ended slavery without spilling a drop of blood). There is a good argument to be made that Canada won the War of 1812 as it successfully repulsed four American invasions and solidified its independence from the United States. It is no wonder that on any summer day in almost any Canadian town, most families fly the Canadian Maple Leaf proudly from their front porch.*

Sailing the Course

For fifteen years I've sailed the course
Across Lake Erie back and forth
Surviving the sun and flies and one knot breeze
The northwest gales and ten foot seas
Night crossings and that quiet peace

We were doing six knots at sunset under sail
Dave Brubeck on the tapes and fried chicken from the pail
We laughed and talked from the windward rail
The night was dark and the stars so clear
The beer was cold and paradise near.

Later at Port the pub was full and the ale flowed free
Old friends and new friendships are there to see
We note the absence of friends and their empty spaces
We lose a few but we gain new faces

The first week of July is a joint celebration
Friendships renewed and Kettle Creek the destination
Some racers will win and others will lose with grace
But we'll each cross the Lake at our own chosen pace
For its not about flags or a trophy for the case
It's the people—all of us—and not the friggin race

The Prime of the Ancient Mariner

(for our dear friend and teacher Carl Anderson, with apologies to Samuel Coleridge)

There stood the Ancient Mariner and looked something like a sage
Some said he was near eighty but couldn't be near that age
The glint in his eyes and summer skies were just about the same
A reflection from the lake he loved and that from whence he came
From the American coast he sailed just eight hours before
With his good friend and companion he named the *Pinafore*

As he walked into the Inn on a dark and stormy night
A fresh breeze blew, the shadows grew and the candles burned more bright
He stepped spryly around the drunks sprawled across the floor
And sat upon a bar stool, neither stiff, nor bent, nor sore
He said "If you buy me a beer" in a voice so clear and sublime
"I may in time give up the secret of the Ancient Mariner's Rhyme"
We gathered quickly around him but he said nothing more
Until he sipped his ale and thus began his tale
Of his life, and Maggie and the Pinafore

His boat was fast with a sturdy mast and as good as any friend
She'd start out slow but in a blow, she raced well in the end
He loved the beamy reach with a boom that touched the stay
He could outreach any boat on any windy day.

He loved to heel the boat through 40 odd knot gales
Under spinnaker, and blooper and fully hoisted sails
Half submerged,
with his crew frantic with busy cockpit bailing
he'd shout into the spray with wild boyish glee
"There's nothing better than a life of sailing"
But his crew got rather green, not making it to lee

The glint in his eyes grew brighter as he gave us his precious time
But we were impatiently waiting for the Old Mariner's Rhyme
But he smiled and said "Patience, and I'll have another ale"
So we quickly bought him one and one again and he continued with his tale
He talked of surfing sideways down waves at eighteen knots
He spoke fondly of all the kids that he helped out quite a lot
Of Sea Scouts and Teaki and Caribbean charters
With George and Terry and other ancient old-time farters

He told of days becalmed and the torment of biting flies
His suffering under blazing skies were left to our surmise
Of beating and tacks that seemed to always cracked the door
For yet another blue flag for the valiant *Pinafore*
And we bided our time for the treasure of the Old Mariner's Rhyme
He talked of construction cranes and spring launches with some dopes
Who always tried pushing but never pulling the damn ropes
Remembering the launches he laughed as he roared
When that boat hits the water I want four guys there on board
He took pity with lawyers whom he thought the most awkward fledgling
And winked when he spoke of his secret midnight dredging

He finished his fourth ale as the hour grew late
It was long past our bedtime but we had swallowed his bait
Please tell us we begged him of the Old Mariner's Rhyme
It was only two thirty and we still had plenty of time
After buying him 4 ales we couldn't just fail
We demanded the secrets of the old Mariner's Grail

The lumber was creaking on the old wooden floor
As he got up and walked, turning back at the door
He said "thanks for the ale and hearing my tale
But it may not be time to give up the Old Mariner's Rhyme
For I have more sailors to train and hurricanes to sail
I have more races to win and mountains to climb
And, frankly, I'm just at the start of my prime"

" But since you've been nice I'll throw you this bone
You're quite capable of finding the Rhyme on your own
The next time it blows a forty knot gale
Take a spouse or a friend and go for a sail
Take a bottle of wine as the sun sets in the west
And remember that life is always the best
On a beam reach"

He stepped out the door and said nothing more
As he walked in the dark back to his *Pinafore*
But you could hear him roar back through the night oh so black
" If you pups are up at half past five I'll race you all back
And beat you alive!"

Carl Anderson was another great character in the club. He sailed until he died at age 82, and continued to ski after 80 (it was free). He was the dean of the yacht club, a perfect gentlemen and great sailor, he trained generations of kids to sail on his boat Pinafore. No weather was too bad for Carl to sail in and there were many times when he shamed the rest of us into racing when we thought the winds were too strong.

Zen of Sailing

There is more to sailing than just sailing the boat. There is a lot of maintenance: changing oil and fuel filters, fixing leaks, cleaning, repairing and replacing broken items, and more. I enjoy this other part of sailing despite the occasional bloody knuckles and other frustrations. I have learned the insides of my boat and the boat has the bloodstains to prove it.

I estimate one hour of sailing for every five or so of maintenance. It is the total experience and I would not change anything. But I do wish I was better at it.

I know the wonders of sailing a broad reach
Less so the whims of the wind gods whom I've known to beseech
The after sail glow at dockside with a wee bit of gin
And the beauty of friendship at the Kettle Creek Inn.

I've sailed through screeching wind and thundering skies
Through drifters with midges and black biting flies
And the worst sound of all that only an engine can make
When it simply just dies…. and so does your wake.

Yes, I confess I've come to it late
Forever avoiding it but confronting my fate
To face the mysterious, evil and tyrannical
Some say the obstinate and somewhat satanical
I can only whisper the demon, the sailboat mechanical.

A knotmeter that suddenly goes on the blink
Oh God, what's that coming up through the sink?
Why's that water sloshing so over the floors?
Torn halyards, loose rudders and jammed bathroom doors
Soft decks, and leaks, frayed wires and more.

But these turmoils are nothing but to challenge your wit
Fixing is good for the soul, I give you no shit.
Is there a sound sweeter than a winch that's been recently greased
Only the moans of a lawyer the mechanic has fleeced.

The victory is sweet when you pull a stripped screw
Or unthread a rusted nut that's been bothering you
The achievement is great—can you want anything more
But to find an old rag and wipe your blood from the floor.

And, is there a better sound I hesitate to mention
Then the wonderful sound of a new diesel engine
And is there a more beautiful sight to be found
Than the wife and the kids disembarking and kissing the ground?
And, I'm sorry Bill but I really can't stop
But the boat really moves well with Terry's old prop.

So its great fun to fix things that fall off of kilter
Although truthfully I can do little more than change a fuel filter
So I've joined the cult to fight evil and demons satanic
And become I confess a born again sailboat mechanic
So here's to you the mechanical shamans and to the toolkits you tote
Is there anything so wonderful as to work on a boat? *

* *Thanks to Kenneth Grahame, "WInd in the Willows"*

The Heron's Song

(apologies to Edgar Allen Poe)

Forty times I heard the halyard clang
In the still of night when the breeze was slight
Forty times more I heard the halyard clang
But the heron just smiled and never sang

Heron please sing your song we cried
But he just flapped his wings and began to fly
There were no lyrics and there was no rhyme
And the halyard forty times again began to chime.

The heron lit upon a bar stool and there he nestled
his face serene but his thoughts were wrestled
resolved, towards me he began to lean
and whispered, "let me tell you what I mean"

Each day is special each one to cherish
Some live for tomorrow and others perish
Each day is worthy of its own celebration
because life is the elixir of our inebriation

The lake we love is a special place
And we race the race despite our pace
Some boats are slow, the perennial caboose
Who's kidding whom, the race is just an excuse

We love our friends on the northern shore
Do we need to race to make this sail more?
Port Stanley is great and so is their beer
So why do we gather only once every year?

Once a year for forty years doesn't make a race
Without each other its…. just another time and place
Has there ever been a sailing group of yore,
" No," quoteth the heron, "nevermore, nevermore!"

Stonehenge

We are the new druids
The fluid druids and leeward stewards
Of the Kettle Creek Inn our celestial Stonehenge
The walls and the floors exude stale beer but also sweet memories
That we inhale and consume and recreate
With every collective breath
We drink lots of ale but what intoxicates
Is the love and friendship we have for each other.
We are a diaspora driven by the wind
And collected by the wind
The scattered and prodigal progeny of Lake Erie
We rise from winter slumber to gather here
To celebrate life
At a solstice of our own choice.

Through our veins course the sunshine and sea, and spray, and soft breezes
And beam reaches
Balancing carefully the delights of our destination
With the joy of the journey and the joy that we share together
Forging friendships that are seasoned with sail and good ale
Running deeper than the waters of Lake Erie
Driven by forces more powerful
Than the winds that collect us and bring us to this shore
And as magical as life itself

We will keep our light lit at this hallowed place
Reminding those who come after us
That a kind and kindred clan of sailors
Met here annually at the seasons zenith
To beseech those that would hear us
To keep the waters and breezes of Lake Erie
Fresh and strong and full of life.

The Women of Sail

(Author's note: the women of sail thought the poem exaggerated their finer points and opted instead for the "bitches of boating"). The truth remains there are no classier women than those who sail with us at AYC.

The women of sail are a special breed
They sometimes follow or take the lead
Biting flies and storms and thirty knot breezes
No matter our mistakes they let us believe
That we do well our skippering and crewing
And that we know something about what the hell we are doing

These women of sail put up with a lot
On windless days when we sail but a knot
She'll say she's no hiker but only a boater
And don't you think it may be time for the motor
Despite the gas and common sense we all seem to lack
Each spring like the tulips they seem to come back

But the women of sail are so much more than the show
They're our helmsman and trimmers wherever we go
They steer by the stars and make inner ticks flicker
They drop anchors, tell tales, and hold their own liquor
They are good sailors who know to live is to imbibe
And they dance gracefully with poles on a spinnaker jibe

These women of sail are not two dimensional
So many interests I'll try just to mention
Some are artists with painting and screens
Others make drives and chip onto greens
Some play tennis with strong topspin serves
Some cycle through Africa to test muscle and nerve
Some tend to gardens and others work for a living
But they always find time for a little extra giving

So the women of sail wherever you hail
Please keep finding time in your lives to come out and sail
We give our love and gratitude and our many thanks
Before we leave port please check the fuel in the tank.

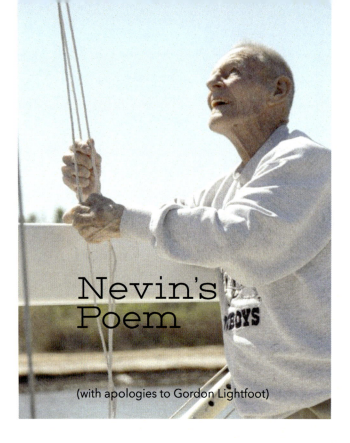

Nevin's Poem

(with apologies to Gordon Lightfoot)

His legend has grown from Vermillion on down
Through Mentor and Erie and Stanley
On Florida beaches and Lake Erie beam reaches
In bars and when hard fast aground
We gather our beers and we give him good cheer
And toast to his good name and good fortune.

As the old sailors go, Nevin's older than most
Some say he's well into his eighties
Although his vision is fading and the teeth are long gone
He still can tease breezes and young ladies

When a younger man he'd beat to weather all day
To find a pub where the night he would stay
But older and sober he was once heard to say
To weather its better to go Chevrolet.

Does anyone know where the love of God goes
When the keg runs empty and dry
With hardly a blink Nevin never misses a drink
And recycles old beer from cans in the sink.

In the old Kettle Creek he still holds his court
As well as his gin, his scotch and his port
He'll sit by the trellis and be his most zealous
That he wants to be shot by a husband most jealous

To the Mouse, Revisited

(With apologies to Robbie Burns)

The best laid schemes of mice and men
Oft go awry time and again
And leave us naught with grief or pain
A broken shackle and a blown out main

Whether to live or sail you take the chance
If upon stars and waves you wish to dance
There is no certainty I guarantee
The weather is never what NOAA said it would be.

The forecast may call for a gentle breeze
Of sunny skies and two foot seas
Always watch the weather is the rule of thumb
But who knew from whence that storm would come

Our boats are made of many pieces
Names and uses to frustrate and tease us
Pins that bend, rigging flying through the air
Untethered sails and booms, that feel of low despair
The stuffing box leak and an engine that seizes
These are a few things that can turn into feces.

No telling the mistakes of skipper and crew
Tacking the jenny to its head or its clew
The spinnaker is flying but the pole's on the deck
Who can think straight when I'm yelling like heck
And who's to blame that we're out of gas too
But somehow together we muddle on through

Of course we should our boats prepare
To cross the lake in weather fair
We mere mortals who seek naught to chance
Know ye better as we look askance
When shit happens
We sail by the seat of our pants

Friends

Of the many trips I like to make
The best is 48 miles across the lake
Clear waters more than 80 feet deep
A night sail to Stanley and promises to keep
Infinite lessons in life to be learned
Perceptions are burst and upside down turned

Leaving the harbor our sails flying and unfurled
We leave the routine of our self-centered world
Slipping into darkness a brief moment of dread
Overcome by the beauty of stars overhead
Reflecting the vast mysteries of life and eternity
We confront and overcome our fears and uncertainties
Of an untamed lake with a stiffening breeze
To head towards a shore we cannot see
Falling short of where we wanted to be

So in a universe and uncertainties without end
Who can underestimate the value of friends
The love and the laughter that forges and mends
Sometimes with some help from a shaker of gin.

Traditions

What is this sailing weekend about
That overcomes our judgment and removes our doubt
Twenty miles out I still sit and wonder
To lightning flashes and the sound of thunder
The marine forecast we ignore and flout

For these questions my mind has one answer
As I sail into squalls like a stumbling dancer
Why go sailing under such terrible conditions
Only one word comes to mind: tradition.

After two props and a burned out boat
What is it that keeps Bobulsky afloat?
Sailing with Bob Lee is legend and lore
What keeps Phyllis returning for more.

The origins of tradition are always murky
What is Thanksgiving without a turkey
Why is it at Passover the youngest shall read
Why do we celebrate Mardi Gras with colored glass beads?
What is it about Halloween that generates fear
Why on St Patrick's day do we color our beer?

This is our tradition much the same
Compared to the others, not quite as tame
We may suffer more I cannot deny
Fighting wind and waves and biting black files
Soaked to the bone under a fifty foot mast
How much longer will this thunderstorm last
A sudden gust and a precipitous heel
Oh my god, I just saw our keel

This is our tradition make no mistake
Undeterred by power boats and gales on the lake
We celebrate life without fossil fuels
We sail in light air more stubborn than mules
Our boats are maintained without getting too frilly
And we now accept things that once scared us silly

From Buffalo to the Detroit River foundries
We thrive on a friendship that defies national boundaries
One last tradition we do without fail
Please raise your glass and toast with an ale

Caol Ila Gael

(with apologies to Peter, Paul and Mary)

Caol ila was a houseboat
She stayed near the pier
She never went racing
Never sailed on her ear

Oh the day dawned quite rainy
Beer stacked high on the fridge
When she tore from her docklines
For the eight o'clock bridge

Oh the lightening was flashing
And the wind it did howl
If Lorraine was aboard
The air would be foul

Oh the mainsail was hoisted
And the jenny unfurled
She sliced through the water
Like the end of the world.

The boat lurched to the starboard
The waves were a plenty
The shelves were soon emptied
As she heeled more than twenty

Oh the TV went crashing
Shit dumped all over the floor
The cushions were soaking
With Forty six miles more

Oh I surveyed the damage
This much I confess
I should not have gone drinking
I should have cleaned up my mess

Caol ila is a raceboat
She runs with the best
But I'm seeking this winter
To become a house guest.

Ode to Lake Erie

The forecast was light wind at 10 knots or less
An omen for smooshed flies that leave quite a mess
Drifters in circles under a hot burning sun
A wicked laugh from my wife, "honey have fun!"

A reporter stopped by who wanted to talk
What is the purpose, tell me a reason why
To sunburn for hours under a hot blazing sky
Crawling so slowly quicker to walk

Maybe it's the lake 10,000 years old
That challenges the sailors both timid and bold
Once covered by glaciers more than one mile high
Defiled by man but defiant and refusing to die

The sound of water rushing under the hull
The vastness of the lake to ponder and mull
The motion of the boat as it accelerates and heels
The wind in your face and how great it can feel
No matter life's losses and pain, the lake always heals.

The halyards and sheets that trim and haul up the sails
No worries as to whether the engine starts up or fails
The boat in the water in the afternoon sun
Knowing that you and your boat have now become one

Come to the lake as a curious child
To appreciate its beauty, untamed and still wild
The lake lives on and continues to teach
To hell with the forecast, catch a spinnaker reach

Ghosts of the Old Kettle Creek Inn

I don't know where the old sailors gathered
Before the pilgrimage to the Kettle Creek
But something is here to us all that speaks
That we are here is all that now matters.

Those who came before well knew
The magic working within this lake
They challenged the lake gods with boat and crew
And taught us to learn from their mistakes.

If we are quiet their voices are heard
Go sail the lake and stay away from the herd
When you find your own breeze take it as far as it goes
You were meant to be free
Like a leaf on the wind, don't ask where it blows.

On sunny days where the breezes are fair
Remember at noon that it's five oclock, somewhere
On launch days when dealing with lawyers and dopes
Remind them to pull and not push on the ropes.
And remember on those rainy, cold and windy days
Sometimes its better to weather in an old Chevrolet
And when drinking some beer to determine its fate
Ask whether it will settle your stomach, or settle your estate.

Their shadows still linger in this hallowed place
After lights last traces fade with the setting sun
Reliving sunny skies and windswept races
Biting flies and sunburned faces
Surfing down waves on a spinnaker run
They disdain the spotlight and our veneration
But make no mistake
The Smithwicks has been passed to the next generation.

Blessed are the Little things

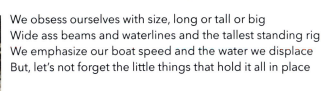

We obsess ourselves with size, long or tall or big
Wide ass beams and waterlines and the tallest standing rig
We emphasize our boat speed and the water we displace
But, let's not forget the little things that hold it all in place

They are pretty inconspicuous on a boat of any size
They are difficult to see with even telescopic eyes
Don't let their insignificance give you any pause
He who ignores the little things may sink from many flaws

Little hose clamps may cost about a dollar each
Inattention or neglect may many lessons teach
On your stuffing box or through-hulls, make doubly sure you got 'em
For a missing clamp or leaky hose will put you on the bottom

Cotter pins have knobby ends
And legs that backward bend
They go hand in hand with clevis pins
Like olives, ice and a bottle of gin.

When you see a mast, straight and proud and tall
Remember it's a simple cotter pin
That keeps it free from fall
When you move the gear shift to go forward or back aft
It is the simple cotter pin that keeps the prop on the shaft
And to motor forward or backwards you are only able
To shift with pins attached to ends of a shiny gear shift cable

It is the little things that always add so much
A vase of flowers on a boat, a simple little touch
A stream of galley water, clean and foot pumped fed
A roll of toilet paper in a clean and working head
Working on the little things from the beginning until the end
On boats or golf or gardens, or whatever you tend to tend
The simple touch and smile of others, what makes a friend a friend

To praise the little things could be a simple hymn
God must have made so many because he most loved them
To add and paraphrase the Sermon on the Mount
Blessed are the little things, the things that really count.

Boat Gossip

Author's note: this poem was written just after our good friend Nevin died. In his last year, you could find him every day near the docks in his red chevy truck, sipping coffee and taking it all in.

Sails on the horizon come slowly into view
The skippers are invisible and so too are their crew
One by one under the bridge the slowly pass
Port Stanley and Ashtabula, the international PSASS

No need for navigation, the old boats know the way
For how long they have done it, none of them will say.
The old boats are the workhorses to and fro across the lake
Always on the lookout for anyone to take

After the race is over, and the boats are safely moored
The docks get dark and quiet and the boats a little bored
Their choice of drink and talk is something of a toss up
But its always fun to listen in on a little sailboat gossip

Pinafore has a new traveler and a boom that doesn't sag
Who'd of thought with Carl gone that boat could win a flag
And *Red Dog*, of course, continues to sail and race
It's such an infectious smile that lights up Bonnie's face

And *Kahuna*, a rocketship and a leader without failing
Find the damn finish, pass a beer, and please keep on bailing
And then there's *Tenspot* with brightly oiled teak
Too bad she has no room to stand, or poop or take a leak

Talisman, what fine seamanship and technique
Always turns sailing heads with such a fine physique
Full sails and ownership with Dominique and Shawn
A full breeze and spinnaker and they are simply gone.

And *Night Music*, more glamorous than a queen
No working stove or oven but always such haute cuisine
And *Travellers* sailing faster with Bob and fearless crew
As long as he is patient and tells them what to do

And *Fat Lady*, last night the hour that she crept in?
A nine thirty start because for three hours she slept in.
Epiphysis, thank God that Alan does the steering
Its also lucky for him that he's become a little hard of hearing.

Three Davids came over on a Hunter named *Cheers*
it takes two of them to keep young David from drinking all the beers.
And Larry and Tami had quite the fun
Watching Bob and Jane steer and salute the sun

And *Renegade*, under a full moon named and born
Who was that woman near midnight soloing on air horn
For cruising no boat alive can beat *Manganinnie*
She can really kick ass flying both a main and jenny

Ma Cherie is a fast boat and Jan is quite divine
I don't know which is better, Charlie or his wine
Rapscallion is sleek and no Spanish galleon
She is pretty frisky and a match for any stallion
Quick and pretty is our fair *Ballisage*
With a click of the motor she led the entourage

Of *Vertigo* and *Whipporwill*, there are oh so many tales
Why is it that always one will motor while the other goes by sail
Do they flip a coin for head or for tails
And who is that red boat that beats their Canadian tails

And then there's *Southern Cross*, with a rating we all dread
Its funny how Anne is tan and Wilson quite red
And what more can be said about Karen and Dennis
Just find a cigar and a full pint of Guinness

These tales continue on
Until the first light of dawn
No boat can be spared from the muck
But the boats quiet down when they hear an old sound
Of a beat up and familiar red chevy truck
The truck and the boats spend a few moments together
Until the truck reminds them, its still better to weather
To go Chevrolet
Then disappears quietly into the bright light of day.

Tenspot

This poem is about our racing boat Tenspot, owned by five partners. Tenspot is a Tartan Ten, about 33 feet long and is a pure racing boat. There is no head, no galley and no refrigerator. It leaks, and there is nothing comfortable about her. But she is a great racing boat and is full of spirit.

Several years ago, my aunt crossed over to Port Stanley on Tenspot, and wrote a poem about her experience that began with, "Tenspot is a very fine sloop, but with no place to poop." I forgot where I put that poem and forgot about defending our Tenspot until somebody referred to her as a Ferrari. Really! Tenspot is more comfortable than a Ferrari, uses less gas and is a hell of a lot more fun.

Our boat *Tenspot* is nothing too plush
Rather Spartan inside with no toilet to flush
Her deck and her topsides are pretty well marred
Thirty years of hard racing has left her well scarred

A mainsail without crinkle and a jenny well blown
One more indication of the miles she's flown
No galley or water and you pee over the side
But like so much in life, the beauty is inside

An AYC PHRF boat she may be one of the last
She sails like a youngster and her ride's a real blast
She's won at the Arts Center and a week at the Bay
And won cases of Arnies best Chardonnay
She's raced out of Cleveland and ports further west
To Stanley and Mentor she's still one of the best

At her age some find it easier to stay at the dock
Just take it easy and run out the clock
But Tenspot's no quitter as long as she floats
She's a spirit and mindset not simply a boat

Whenever the wind blows she's ready to go
With or against the prevailing flow
She flies high to windward in seven foot seas
Snatching each lift or a shift from a stiffening breeze
Under spinnaker she's prone to jump to the lead
Surfing down waves at 20 knot speed

When the docks are deserted and the people long gone
I'll stop by in the evening to just hang around
I contemplate the boat and the winds she's been through
Always giving her all and protecting her crew
I marvel at the boat, there really isn't much to her
But she's never faltered or balked, always a doer

Some skeptics may say she's nothing but glass
Something to ride but hard on your ass
I love and admire her and how she keeps it together
Through spinnaker jibes and beats in stiff weather

She's quieted as I tuck her in for the night
I turn to leave and she is soon gone from my sight
She will wake when the winds rise and the windex swings north
And tug at her lines to boldly sail forth.

Square Pegs and Round Holes

In an attempt to level the playing field, racing boats use a PHRF handicap system, which factors into a complicated formula sail area, beam, draft, a "J" Measurement, and an eye of newt to take into account different designs. PHRF ratings are probably a good concept but the details can get shaky. Some racers become too obsessed with PHRF ratings, forgetting that performance is the key and depends so heavily on teamwork.

Make no mistake she is a Great Lake
We sail her together and we know what it takes
We forego a big engine and a boat air conditioned
Raise sails, trim sheets and broach in stiff winds
We tack and we jibe under a windex that spins
But the winds have just led us back to where we have already been.
We do it the hard way, time and again
We are brothers and sisters and the Lake is our kin

Yet we are different as each other's boats
Some bang around buoys and some drink while afloat
Some are light and fast with hot racing sails
Some serve fine food in the cockpit and don't sit on the rails
Some boats drink wine and others dark brew
Some have old crew and some are brand new
Be we are children of the Lake with our own special grace
And none is defined by how we finish a race

PHRF ratings can be grating as we all surely know
Some sail to their rating and some well below
Some like to point and others to reach
It's the same lesson to learn and then again teach

We are diverse with reds, yellows and greens
Not in black or in white, but a lot in between
We can't quantify performance with numbers that fit in
The people who "win" must dig deeper within
Each race can be different and more often than not
A high or low PHRF rating doesn't mean squat.

This race is a tradition, we must never forget
Much larger than us or the PHRF rating we get
Years from now no one will remember the race
But, will know us by our style and our grace
That we meet here, each year, at this time hallowed place
To toast to each other and every new face
So take your Smithwicks held high in your glass
Here's to one and to all, and a kick in our ass.

Sailing on a Great Lake

Lake Erie has got some bad press through no fault of its own. Instead, it is our fault that the Lake has been long associated with the "rust belt:" industrial decay, burning rivers, pollution, a dying lake and perpetual snow from November to April. But the Lake has comeback and supports a broad diversity of life. There is no better way to experience Lake Erie, or any body of water, than on a sail boat.

Sailing on Lake Erie has a magic and poetry all its own. From the moment the engine is turned off and the sails are raised, the boat begins to heel a little and move forward, magically. Gliding quietly through the water, the sailor becomes one with the boat, the breeze, and the water as the boat seemingly takes flight. Distinctions blur as awareness awakens feelings numbed by the frustrations and stresses of the week. The moment becomes paramount: stresses are washed out and cleaned in the bubbly wake of the boat, discarded for another day, and then simply forgotten.

The Lake has much to offer, revealing herself to only those who take the time to know her. Sailing is slow, painfully slow to those obsessed with arriving at a destination and overlooking the journey. To sail the Lake means to know the Lake intimately because sailing is slow. The Lake is not a one night stand.

Sailing is quiet. Sailing offers a remarkable opportunity to observe cormorants diving for fish, to participate in gentle conversation, contemplate life's greater mysteries, or simply take a nap in the sun.

Sailing Lake Erie creates a healthy perspective. As much as we may like to think we can adapt the world to our needs, it is really the world to which we must adapt. The Lake is bigger than us, more powerful than us, and we accept these terms when we venture onto the Lake. The Lake is well worth it.

Dreams of Hot Coffee at the Perk

Before the Sunday race, we usually meet for coffee and a bagel at the Harbor Perk in Ashtabula Harbor. It's a great place with better and less expensive coffees than Starbucks, and a great ambience. The owner, Jake, gets a lot of credit for bringing something this simple and classy into the harbor, and it seems to be working as the whole harbor district is undergoing a renaissance.

It was Sunday and time for a race, but
The Lake was in a mood
No frolic in her play
The waves were big and the winds
Strong and relentless
It was one of those days, either
Stay warm at the Perk with coffee and bagel
Or face the Lake on terms not of our choosing
But we are sailors and we chose the Lake

The beats upwind were wet and painful
The wind knocked the boat down, buried
Its leeward deck in angry green water
Stiff figures, huddled on the high side,
Clad in yellow and red storm gear, struggling
To sit upright arms wrapped in lifelines
Their weight overwhelmed by the force of wind,
Which heeled the boat more as the wind grew

As the bow rose high to meet each oncoming wave
Reaching the crest, balancing precariously for only a moment
Then sliding, plunging into a dark trough
Only to surface again, spray whipped by the wind
And we cursed the wind
But never the Lake
From under sheets of cold water,

Downwind, deceived by a false calm
As we sailed fast with a faster wind
We raised our spinnaker, dead downwind
Pole back to the portside shrouds
Boom forward to the starboardside shrouds
Surfing, corkscrewing down mountainous waves
At crazy speeds
Bending the very wood in the stressed tiller
Its side bulging

Foredeck, setting poles and untangling lines
Trimming a wild sail while trying to balance, standing
Grinding winches with tired aching arms
No kids here, just guys over 60
Hanging on, working together
Anticipating and recovering from broaches and puffs
And Jeanne, grinding away on the low side
She had voted for coffee and bagels
At the Harbor Perk.

In the end, we survived
And won the race but not a trophy
BFD
Excellence is its own reward
And is too often overlooked

Excellence that begins with a group of aging sailors
Whose peers stayed in bed, or played
A round of golf
Something more suited for their age

A group of old guys (when did that happen to us?)
Working together as a team
As we have for twenty years
Together
Each knowing what to do
And when to do it.
Trusting each other
Knowing that the whole is greater
Than the sum of its parts
Trying to forget
that it is warmer and more comfortable
With coffee and a bagel at the Perk.

Old guys on an old boat.
She is 35 years old and the racing scars to prove it
And built solid without frills and comfort
Mast held up with 3/8 inch wire and chainplates,
Hull held together with thin plywood bulkheads,
But loved and maintained and cared for
Imagine the stress on this boat
The forces in the water and in the wind
Bearing down unrelenting
Seeking to destroy it
But failing
Because she challenged the Lake, held together
And won.
Surrounded by deep water, and the deep love of her crew
Buffeted by fierce winds,
Becoming One with the Lake and the wind.

And we, in return, huddled,
On a ten foot wide deck 33 feet long
Surrounded by deep and vast amounts of water
And buffeted by fierce winds
and cold spray in our faces
Became one with each other
Became one with the Boat
And the Lake and the wind.
All working together.

And that is why we race
And dream of hot coffee at the Perk.

The Day of the Dog

(or Cardhu's Lament)

*This poem chronicles a race between our old boat Cardhu, and
Red Dog, owned and skippered by Art Benson*

The sun rose red, a sailor's dread
Light force fed into our throbbing head
Flags and halyards dead, without a breath of air
River scum floated upstream without a care
We crawled from our bunks all stiff and spent
Eyes bloodshot, our lairs stank of stale grog
As the sun and air lifted our inebriated fog
How was I to know that thus began *Cardhu's* lament
And the glorious day of the *Dog*.

It was the 18th of June of '95
The wind had died but would soon revive
The *Dog* looked sleepy and tired that muggy morning
But the signs were there and I missed their warning
For its bottom was sobered and its crew was too
Iced in the cooler a case of Lift Bridge brew

Her skipper farted, belched and rambled
His wife and crew to windward scrambled
As the *Dog* motored out there was such a view
As his wife and crew scrambled anew, and anew
You can see why our confidence grew
And why we steered to windward too.

The race began as the morning winds grew
Victory was ours or so we thought we knew
The *Dog* broke off and sailed toward shore
A trolling fisherman he tried to duck
But cut its lines as she pushed her luck
While we preferred windward and offshore
Where the fishermen swore less and the winds blew more
We rounded Redbrook and set our chute in style
We relaxed, we had the *Dog* by a country mile
Glancing back we could only stop and stare
In awe and wonder as the *Dog* was still there
Gaining, flying every sail and urging his crew
While his fleet footed wife and crew scrambled anew

We rounded Outer Vic's with the *Dog* at 40 yards bare
We tacked and tacked with Olympic flair
Grinding winches and jumping to leeward with care
Overrides and holes, salty curses wrent the air
But after a half dozen tacks the *Dog* beat us fair
We dipped our flags to her all stunned and groggy
To honor this persistent gas powered Doggy

After generous amounts of gin and vermouth
I cannot end here without telling the truth
I have analyzed carefully and twice taken stock
Her skipper's ability I cannot belie
To beat the *Dog* you must sink her at the dock
Or let sleeping Dogs to leeward lie

Midnight Through the Pelee Passage

This was written in 2007 after I sailed with some friends on their new boat Night Music from Lake St. Clair to Ashtabula, a wonderful ride down the Detroit River with a 4 knot current into Lake Erie and through the Pelee Passage about midnight.

Basking in the warmth
of the afternoon sun and good friends
A full main and steady engine
and a four knot current
Sweeping us down narrow channels on the Detroit River
past decaying factories long abandoned
and barren islands with faded warning signs
into the welcoming waters of Lake Erie
a rebirth, a baptism, a new beginning.

Sun setting behind the Fermi power plant
east from the Detroit light into growing dusk
Sounds of water lapping against our bow
and a fall breeze singing softly in the rigging,
we have heard all day,
gather a new intensity and become Night Music
as the first star begins to dance above

Midnight through the Pelee Passage
Billions of stars and unseen black holes
dancing in unison above the mast and spreaders
with our companions and the world around us
to the gentle harmonies of Night Music

The twinkling lights above the mast
sisters to the blinking lights on the water,
marking unseen reefs and shoals
or the bow of a freighter five hundred yards away
and closing,
swaying silently to the melody of Night Music

A full moon peeks shyly above the horizon
beautiful daughter of the Lake
Slowly rising to her feet
she hesitates and then joins the cosmic dance
to the pulsating rhythms of Night Music.

Too soon comes the first light of dawn
the dancers begin to fade and then disappear
The sounds of a diesel engine are heard once again
the bright glare of the morning sun on the water
But Night Music somehow remains
Suspended in time and space
To be reborn, once again,
When good friends gather on the waters of a great Lake
reflected in a night sky with billions of stars.

Dunkirk Ghost

He walked onto the dock
Under the cloud of a passing storm
Thunderstorms, wind and heavy rain
A wizened old sailor
With creases from beating into many a headwind
Stooped and bent and walked with a cane
He stepped of his boat and with a voice still strong
Accepted our offer of an old single malt
With a warm smile and easy grace.

He talked of the present
of a night passage through the Canal
A few hours sleep
And a stormy ride from Port Colborne
Speaking nothing of his past or future

Finishing his drink he thanked his hosts
And disappeared quickly into the misty night
The boat was gone before mornings first light
Was he just another sailor, or Dunkirk's sailing ghost.

Simplicity of Sail

There is a simplicity I find and take
Whenever I sail upon the Lake
Whether a fifty cent key on a propeller shaft
Or the seagull who knows and seems to laugh

The simplicity of sail is easy to find
Let the sounds of the water replenish your mind
Let your face feel the breeze
And your back bask in the sun
Your stresses will ease
But you're not quite yet done.

Add friends and some gin to this curious batch
A moment of zen and watch it all hatch
Sailing six knots is a really good speed
Who would have guessed that's all you would need.

When was the last time a vacation you took
And getting there was better than the place you had booked
Or played a song and listened to the words
Or woke in the morning up to the music of birds
Cable tv can be really nice
But what do you need more than some gin on cold ice

When was the last time you tweaked
A week of vacation into three long weeks
When was the last time you spent all night
Climbing through your boat for a bilge filling leak.

Dinner can be just a bowl of cold beans
Funny it's the simple stuff that goes neglected and unseen
And becomes important, what's more to say
Have you examined your coupling key today?

This poem was inspired a few years ago during a summer cruise to Presque Isle. Manganinnie, (Terry and Jeanne Persily), engine running, slowed and stopped moving altogether. We investigated. Deep within the bowels of the sailboat, in cramped and confined spaces that never see sunlight and few owners, the engine/transmission is connected by a coupler, held by a fifty cent bronze key, to the propeller shaft which exits the boat and attaches to the propeller which then propels the boat. The key became dislodged due to a faulty alignment and allowed the shaft to slide out of the coupler, disconnecting the propeller from its power.

It's ironic that a fifty cent bronze key could play such a pivotal role on a 38 foot, 7 ton sailboat. And the boat could have sank had not the zinc on the propeller shaft bumped into the strut and stopped the shaft from sliding out of the boat, leaving a one inch hole in the bottom of the boat.

In another twist, we later determined that the trouble was a .045 inch gap between the coupling and the shaft causing the shaft to wobble. Yes, the clearance was forty five thousandths of an inch when the standard is only five thousands of an inch. I replaced my shaft that winter. Read and re-read the poem "Blessed are the Little Things."

Manganinnie

We have cruised for almost 20 years with Terry and Jeanne Persily on their boat Manganinnie and Jim and Carrie Cozy on their boats Silverheels, Spar Hawk, Silver Lining, and now Talaria.

She lays with her sisters all heaven kissed
Silently sleeping in swirling morning mist
As it gently recedes past trees so heavy and dewey
Past a lonely gull bobbing on a worn painted buoy
Casting light upon night's shadows which still persist
She yearns for the deep water that she can't resist

The sun rose slowly without sound or rancor
Broken only by diesel chugs and the clang of her anchor
Rolling out of bed and grabbing my coat
I banged my head on the hatch and saw the red boat
A grey beard hoisting his mainsail and jenny
Past our mooring came gliding, our sister *Manganinnie*

When we finally make way she is far in the distance
As she ventures forth into the unknown without assistance
Plotting her course to avoid shoals, reefs and rocks
She finds her wind and reserves our docks
Pipes and stars lite as evening fell
A glass of highland scotch to the tunes of Jacque Brel.

Manganinnie legend holds, shall keep the sacred flame
For no one touched by her shall remain the same
Facing storms that toss and seas that can't be crossed
She ventures forward no opportunity lost
Opening wide the waters that close the deepest seas
Splashing her spray high into the air, free
Of self imposed limits to find her own identity

From Erie to Abino or any proper port
She offers her Macallan and holds her court
In a cushioned cockpit with candles bright
She engenders warmth and shares her light
With anyone searching for their beacon in the night
That they may find their own, as is their right
So they too may trust their sight

Dancing on a Wave

Glistening waves rise and fall
Casting long shadows extending to the trough of the following wave
As it rises from the Lake reflecting fading sunlight
Sparkles of sunlight dancing on its crest for one last chance
Before the music stops

The gentle rhythm of the boat is my friend and soul mate
Chasing from my being the vestiges of the madness of the office
Incessant phone calls and demanding people
Shouting, demanding they buy my time
The lake and the boat remind me
My life is not for sale

Beacon on a Darkening Night

The sky deepens in the east as dusk begins to fall
Gently like a tiger lily blossom closing on a summer night
Bright orange contrails burn in an azure sky
No matter our destination, the past is still behind us
Dissolving, even now, into my disappearing wake

Not even the sun stays put in just one place
It leaves for the night and the timing is right
Allowing us to reflect on the day
If only momentary, and it is gone
But the waves continue to break and roll
Easing our minds and soothing our soul
Heeling gently, we reach for the lighthouse blinking in the distance

Last Sail

The last sail of the season
With storm clouds looming
A cold north breeze booming
The boat heels and drives through the seas
Waves crash over the starboard bow
Water pours over the leeward rail
A soft swooshing sound trailing our wake

The jib was trimmed and mainsail reefed
The wind in the rigging whistled
Like a teapot steaming
The water was boiling with frothy whitecaps
Rode the big waves up and down
Burying the bow in the next wave
Smashing into another wave
With such force that the rigging and mast shook
Ice water geysers sprayed high into the air
Drenching us huddled in the cockpit.

Afterwards we reached the harbor shelter
And sails were quickly removed
Within twenty minutes we were back at her dock
Stripped bare of her sails and booms and other adornments
A weather beaten mast all that remains
Except for memories of a last sail
To carry us through a cold and gloomy winter.

Yodi

The late Yodi sailed for many years on Manganinnie. She was a Himalayan and kind of a "fluff" cat and kitty princess. Terry and Jeanne took her many places, three weeks on the cruise and some places too sensitive to disclose. This was a great sailing cat who died a few months after this was written on her last cruise. The history of this poem is that Carrie Cozy caught a bat inside their boat cabin a few nights before (Carrie is real good at catching bats and other little animals). So, for the rest of the cruise, everybody was looking for bats in their belfry.

Yodi is a sailing puss
She's shy and timid but not a woos
She sails in weather both foul and fair
And poops and pukes within her lair.

When the sailing turns too rough, she will let you know
And leave something lumpy and wet on your pillow
A litter box is provided neatly in the quarter berth
She sits and misses but to no-one's mirth
Such an abundance of style and finesse
She still remains a yachting kitty princess

Her attributes are widely admired
Countless felines and humans have been inspired
She may sleep all day but that's alright
She guards Manganinnie alone at night
While others drift off in gentle sleep
She knows her duty and her watch to keep

It was past midnight at the Erie Yacht Club
She sat alone in the darkness without a rub
She heard a noise and looked above
At an intruder to maul the ones she loved

Yodi leaped into action when she heard a loud scream
Its that hysterical woman again can this be a dream
But the woman kept screaming "it's a bat, it's a bat!"
But Yodi knew better, much better than that

The next night it happened all over again
The same evil presence with the same evil grin
Yodi growled and put fear into its sinister heart
And the diabolical guest was soon quick to depart

As most stories go, this one also has legs
Further discussion the truth only begs
Some say it was a bat with features so crude
Some say another cat, just looking for food.

Yodi is not talking for she surely knows
That silence is golden and her legend just grows
She was taught to be quiet, never to brag or to gloat
what happens afloat should always stay on the boat.

To this day, Terry continues to say he saw another cat jump off the boat and walk down the dock. But Yodi always maintained that you could never trust people over 65 that had been drinking scotch

Beautiful Day

A beautiful day
Blue sky and blue water
Steady breeze from the east
I could have flown full sails
        But didn't
Or kept up with the other boats
        But didn't
But I enjoyed the sail, the day and you

What is an hour worth, billed or unbilled
On a beautiful day
What matters time if the pleasure is in the moment
        Each succeeding moment
        Cascading like a waterfall
What is a half knot of speed
Over millions of light years
Or a 40 mile sail.

What the Sailboats Know

Have you noticed how a sailboat relaxes
after a day of sailing a beam reach
beating into the wind
or motoring in flat seas?

Not in a teeming harbor
jammed into a floating trailer park
and strapped down to a concrete dock

But swinging softly in still waters
in a small bay in Presque Isle
at anchor
nose to the wind
inhaling deeply the fresh cool breeze
through open hatches and ports
sighing after every puff
complete content reflected in the water

The sailboats must know something
because they do it all so well
and always with their face to the wind
swinging gently to an fro
in the soft light of late afternoon
listening to WQLN

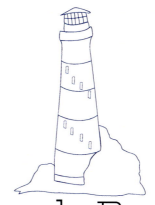

People Poetry

I have inadvertently understated an important part of sailing on Lake Erie: the people who sail upon her waters. Sailors are a special group not because of anything particular but because we share common experiences that begin beyond the breakwall.

Sailing on Lake Erie is an exercise in self discovery, realizing that there is much more we can do than we ever thought possible: we can strive for a distant shore we cannot see beyond the horizon.

Sailors are diverse and incapable of being pigeon-holed into superficial distinctions of politics, religion, class or wealth.

Our diversity comes together in teamwork on a sailboat. We work as a team to prepare our boats for launch. With the help of a crane, we lift and launch 12,000 pound boats working together as a team pulling lines and scurrying to insure that the boat is not damaged as it is lowered into the water. Its not unlike our ancestors 10,000 years ago trying to bring down a giant wooly mammoth with a few rocks and spears.

The teamwork in sailing really comes alive during a race. A good crew size runs from 4–6 people depending on the boat, and each person has an individual job which includes steering, calling tactics, releasing or sheeting in a sail and setting, trimming, jibing and dousing spinnakers. One mistake by anyone can cost a race, damage a sail or even injure another person.

Crew work does not stop when the sails are set; in breezy conditions we all sit on the "high side" to balance and level the boat so it goes faster. Serious racers will sometimes place crew below in the cabin, above the keel, to maintain weight low on the boat. After the race, the crew carefully folds sails, coil line, and cleans the boat for the next race. Afterwards, good crews often drink and dine together with crews from other boats, telling better stories as the night wears on and the keg runs dry.

Non racers also sail their boats in teams. Sometimes the best teams are the husband/wife/significant other teams that handle their boats well in any condition. Boats sail so much better when sailed by teams and not individuals.

Sailors crave the silence when the sails are raised and the engine is turned off. We can hear the sounds of the breeze through the rigging, and the bow parting the water, and the bubbly wake behind us. We can converse without straining our voices, or simply contemplate and become one with the Lake that surrounds us.

Sailors understand that to sail means not to rush or hurry. There is no deadline and there are no schedules to follow. We leave that at our place of work. We appreciate the journey and let the destination come on its own.

There is nothing special about the people who venture beyond the breakwall. Anybody can do it and anyone can learn to handle the challenges of the Lake, the boats and the weather that make sailing so unique.

In the Spring, sailors can get caught in a fog so thick nothing can be seen. Even under sunny conditions most of us have hit bottom, sometimes a rock, mud or a sandbar; and a few have needed help to get off. We've seen jib sheets wrapped around propellers, broken halyards and propellers, broken masts, roundups, knockdowns and "death rolls" under a spinnaker. But we manage to survive it all and, back on the dock and after a few beers, we get some really good stories out of them.

Most importantly, we learn to trust our boat, ourselves and those with whom we sail. We learn to respect each other; the young parents who take small children and their dog out to race around the buoys; a retired elementary principal who soloed down the Intercoastal and into the Gulf on his Tartan 27 with his dog (his wife stayed home but the dog didn't know any better).

On any given dock in almost any given port and at almost any time, we can open up a bottle of fine single malt scotch, play a little Gordon Lightfoot or some Jacques Brel and listen to stories of ordinary people who do amazing (and sometimes really stupid) things on a sailboat, and everyone has plenty of tales to tell.

If there is one thing in my life that's missing
It's the time that I spend alone
Sailing on the cool and bright clear water
There's lots of those friendly people
Showing me ways to go
But I never want to lose their inspiration.

—Cool Change, Little River Band

Phyllis' Poem

At age where many argue for their limitations
Accepting them without lamentation or other hesitations
At a time when many settle into a comfortable rut
In silence with nary a thought nor an and, if or but
At a time when imagination and creativity are lost
And old stories gather and accumulate moss
          You just did it and went to the Pyramids

When many have surrendered their dreams and their vision
For a beer and a sofa and a color television
At a time when wonder and learning are no longer practiced
You have sprouted in a desert and bloomed like a cactus
At a time when people have restricted their thought
You have never asked why but always why not
          And you dumped the ice cubes from your bud light
          Began drinking brown beer and still lost weight

When events and ill winds against you conspire
Remember all of us to whom you inspire
To reach higher and set caution afire
To live every moment and still never tire
We know you've tried hard for the battles you've won
But to know you is to love you, …. And long may you run

The Race

She is pretty and petite
And all around neat
Red wavy hair and eyes hazel green
An infectious laugh and quick with a smile
We sat on the leeward rail and talked for awhile
Who can envision the struggles within and unseen?

Without hesitation she jumped to tend sails
Or called back to the helm a flickering tell tail
She looked out for starboard boats perched on the pulpit
She not only enjoyed it but really did gulp it
She handled it confidently, and calmly with grace
All at Presque Isle on a Wednesday night race

Afterwards relaxing on the boat with a beer
She talked of her illness expressing no fear
Of the hours of chemo and the chronic fatigue
Cancer in the fourth stage, never a good sign
With her face to the wind and her feet on the line
There was never a doubt she was out of my league

The human spirit can be a wondrous thing
Some cower in corners but she chose to take wing
When challenged by cancer
She's become quite the dancer
On sunlit beam reaches in a steady breeze
Or while beating to weather in stiff choppy seas

Whatever the odds, you just fight it like hell
I recall a cartoon that describes her well
About a little frog stalked and about to be eaten
But adamantly refusing to be quietly beaten
The frog thrusts at the bird, the image still lingers
A scrawny but defiant long middle finger

(ps, the frog survives but that is a poem for another day)

The Clan

An early and a favorite poem written in an 18th century house near Inverness in northern Scotland. A group of AYC sailors (six couples) rented a gorgeous house overlooking a beautiful valley only a few miles from Culloden Moor, the site of a British victory over the Scottish clans led by Bonnie Prince Charlie.

I pause upon my lofty loo
Content but attracted to my view
The window rattles and ancient winds blow
Upon silent shrouded moors in mist below

Upon rock strewn hills and jagged crests
Grazing sheep and naked trees at rest
The deepening drizzle swirls on horizons bleak
Parting, revealing its snow capped peaks
And the sun, burning free, that the thistle seeks

Fields of green and brown beneath me spread
Stacked stone fences and hedgerows tinged in green and red
Old stone abbeys encircled by those long dead
What truth they knew such gods they'd seen
Upon this mystical Caledonians scene serene

This land is clanland I've heard them say
From Glen Affric to the Firth of Moray
Frasers, Stewarts, Lovatts and so many more
Believing they met their doom at Culloden Moor
But stayed together then and evermore

Yet from their damp ashes like the Phoenix rose
A new clan from the west, strong and close
Bursting forth each spring from fertile rows
Sprayed from vessels of wind and glass
Well heeled hulls and stiff raked masts
Reefed mains and curling waves in shrieking blows
Yellow clad figures edging stiffly aft
Huddled wet and cold yet the feeling grows
Becoming one with all and with their craft

So I hoist my glass to the people I love
Who look toward tall mountains and the windex above
Who hit long balls and shags on grass links
And walk in mossy forests as the morning sun blinks
Gathering by the fire for company and drinks
Who like daffodils brighten a somber land
And frolic and gambol like newborn lambs
Of this group I pledge to each woman and a man
I'm pleased to be part of you, and you of me
The Ashtabula clan.

The Rime of the Anal Mariner

(even deeper apologies to Samuel Coleridge)

He is the anal mariner, who sailed the lakes alone
Always seeking crew under every unturned stone
He sometimes snared my nephew, always quite a catch
His tennis wife was willing but too often won her match

A sailor bold and brave he always raised his sails
Whether sunny skies or biting flies or those thirty odd knot gales
He oft-times crossed a freighter path we thought to take a look
But there was Bruce in cabin hunched absorbed in just a book

At dockside he was a hermit never stirring from his bunk
He would lay about his boat an unrepentant clump
Unshaven and unshowered like some medieval monk
Emerging to announce, with pride, it was time to take a dump

Going for a walk with Bruce is filled with perils fraught
For Bruce was never shy about expressing any thought
Sometimes he would go cycling on his folding aluminum steed
But he wasn't sure of what to do with nothing there to read

I'll end this parody with a prayer
For our brave lone sailor solitaire
May you always join us for drinks at each day at 5 o'clock
May we always greet you when you arrive at any dock

Ode to My Hurricane Bobe

Everyone, particularly a Gentile like myself, needs a Jewish grandmother, or Bobe (rhymes with puppy). I was fortunate to have been adopted (somewhat) by the greatest of them all. The first was written maybe 10 years ago when she decided to stick out a hurricane at her home in Boca. The second was this past year when she turned 90. I like the second one the best because it catches as much as can be caught of her character, and gives me inspiration as well.

I know a nice bobe from Boca
Who danced to the "horah", not polka
When hurricane flags raised
She hardly seemed fazed
She just added a shot to her mocha

Like pachysandra our brave Alexandra
Decided to lay low for the storm
But as Hurricane Francis drew near
She heard such a chorus of fear
but stubbornly kept true to her form

She heard warnings for the coastals to flee
And an invite from Jeannie that was free
But she disregarded the pleas
And with a smile and a tease
Said "Don't worry I have vodka and brie"

The streets soon had water up to the knees
Poles toppled and trees fell in the 80 knot breeze
But our bobe was dry
and with a twinkle in her eye
said "there's still plenty of vodka and cheese"

We were all quite worried when after three days
Nobody had called as to whether she was okay
But we all let out a big sigh
When we heard that she did not die
And we marveled at her suffering and fortitude
When after the first day her vodka ran dry

Oi Vey!

My birthday wish to my Bobe from Boca

I cannot believe but I heard them say
That my bope is turning ninety today
(or tomorrow or the next day)
This comes with a twist, but I state without guile
I'm so proud of my bope and I'm just a gentile

She is more than the daughter of a famous artist
Look deeper and see there's much more to the gist
For the moon is much less than without the sun
And her father was half without Julia Liekerman
From two great families my Bope did sprout
And that, we should know, is what it's about

She came to America with her parents who brought her
She and Joe would raise three such incredible daughters.
She is more than a survivor and she still continues to bloom
Her warmth and conversation spillover from any-sized room

I love her style and class with her continental charm
Her voice when she's tough would shake a gendarme
She is graceful and kind, and stays in good form
Standing tall without wilting through life's many storms.

What I love most is simply her mind
Always searching for something new and exciting to find
I'm told that she never made it to college
But, oh, what a vast resource of wisdom and knowledge

My Bope may think that she may be growing old
But she will never age as long as she holds
Onto her curiosity and willingness to learn
Her candle will continue forever to burn
I can't think of anything much more to rhyme
So to you, my bope, happy birthday and L'chaim.

Le Hommage Quintessence

My first, and only French poem, to a couple we all got to know from France and their dog Maurice and their sailboat Quintessence. They were transferred to Houston and we had a little dinner party for them before they left.

Nous hommage to Antoine, Maureen and Maurice
Les francais nos amis, mes cheres
As a poet francais I am but a poor amateur
Butchering your language and my pentameter
You struggled to speak our language and learn it you did
I will try to speak yours but you'd better put on the lid.

You blew in from Lac Erie with a le vant nord
To AYC where Bob met you and opened the door
It was a cold autumn day, but you brought vie, chaud and éclair bien
Like a beam reach on a summer day, nous souvien, nous souvien

Le petite bateau, *Quintessence*, wasn't huge
But it overflowed with laughter, and love and du van rouge
How appropriate the name on its stern you mounted
For you knew your boat had was what in life most counted

We meet again at Chez Persily our collective presence
Good friends, good food, good wine–life's quintessence
To bid au revoir to Maurice, Maureen and Antoine
Our time was too short, too soon for you to be gone
But come back and visit soon in the future not distant
Antoine, Marine, Maurice……. and les enfants!

Welcome Home!

A spring evening is difficult to end
on a porch basking in the warmth of good friends
Rain rustling a lush green garden
soothes and softens a mind both frayed and hardened
Fragrances and colors and clusters of spring flowers
amidst tall shady trees that just seem to tower
A simple meal garnished with wine and laughter
worries are forgotten and no longer matter
A slow tasty scotch and a satisfied sigh
time has run out and it's a hard goodbye
Its easier to leave good friends at the end of the day
Knowing that tomorrow is never too far away.

Fellow Travelers

The world in an incredible suduku
Place nine numbers in a box
Watch them grow and morph
A number three dissolves into an eight
And a number six becomes the letter "b"

A crossword puzzle
Where the clues and the answers change
But the letters remain the same
Meaning becomes "no meaning"
And the Buddha smiles

We ride the air currents
High above forested mountains
Catching a lift, sucked down by a downdraft
A rough landing may be waiting for us all

But our fellow travelers remain by our side
Soaring above the sun,
Down the rocky slope to oblivion
And to whatever eternity awaits us
And to you fellow travelers I toast

For Julia

A bar exam is hard to take
Too much to know for just its own sake
Three years of law school to regurgitate
Only a brief glimpse of your chosen fate

A sailing trip after attaining a life time goal
That can bring rewards at a heavy toll
As you learn and practice your legal role
Avoid the temptations and protect your soul

For only so long can anyone continue to litigate
So, make time to love and live and recuperate
A quiet place to regain your dreams and thought
Looking back on battles won and battles lost

Remember Lake Erie and its summer breeze
Rocked to sleep on gentle seas
Warmth and laughter of your dearest friends
Remind us it's the journey and not the ends.

This was written while cruising with the Persilys aboard their boat Manganinnie. They had their niece Julia and fiancé as guests for a few days in Presque Isle after just completing the New York bar exam. They are now happily married and practicing law.

The Women of Sail, Revisited

This next poem was written several years after the first Women of Sail. It was inspired by three of my favorite women of sail. At an age where many women are content to take their grandchildren to the zoo or knit by the fire, these three women embody a spirit of adventure and pushing the envelope to the edge. The first, Jeanne, races regularly with her husband Terry and six more of us on Tenspot–a boat you have to see and still won't believe how basic and primitive it is. Tenspot has no "head," and the rest of the comfort index gets worse from there. But, she is fast and dependable.

One blustery day in October, we were the only three and we decided to race anyway. The image still remains of the boat heeled over at thirty degrees plus, slamming into seven foot waves, tacking back and forth into twenty five knots of a cold north breeze and Jeanne crouched on the low side up to her knees in water and cranking in the headsail.

The other two women, Bonnie and Linda, both lost husbands but continue to take their boats out in almost any kind of weather–often making the 20 mile round trip between Ashtabula and Geneva on the Lake. Bonnie came within a few seconds of winning the overall race to Port Stanley in 2010. In truth, these women represent a much larger group of women who venture into the uncertainty and wildness of Lake Erie and this is a tribute to all of them.

the women of sail have got a little bit older
a little bit greyer but not the less bolder
they still take to the seas
in a twenty knot breeze
no load for them is too big to shoulder

a few still brave the Sunday morning races
thirty degree heels and cold spray in their faces
they grind on the low side with hardly a care
bundled in coats and gloves and long underwear
forsaking a morning of eggs and coffee and finer fare

a few have lost their very best friend
but hesitate not at the first hint of the wind
they carry their sails full and halyards taut
to challenge the Lake is what the Lake has taught
a simple gift, in storms to bow and bend
and never to break

the women of sail dance on waves sparkling in sunlight
a day sail or cruise is always just right
a trip to the strip, friends and laughter
an afternoon dip, an evening nip after
a full day lived and shared, before the backstay splits the moon

the women of sail continue to teach
aging gracefully is within all our reach
follow the wind wherever it blows
enjoy the ride wherever it goes
don't watch life pass from a chair on the beach.

For Ash

One of the best things about cruising on Lake Erie is making and maintaining good friends. I met Ash in 1999 after a sail from Erie to Port Dover, where Ash lived with his wife Mary. Ash was a retired lawyer and belonged to the Port Dover Yacht Club. An aluminum fitting that holds the boom to our mast had broken, and Ash drove me an hour into the Ontario countryside to his friend and blacksmith Klaus, who quickly repaired it. It led to a great friendship.

Ash and Mary became a permanent part of our summer cruise for the past 10 years. We often took his little powerboat into Long Point Bay to fish for perch–we never caught much but Mary always fried our catch for hors d oeuvres. He dabbled in stocks, real estate transactions, woodworking and carving soapstone.

He often sailed a leg with us from Port Dover to Port Colborne where we met more friends. On one such occasion, our spinnaker shackle broke in high winds and seas, and I had to go forward to retrieve the sail from the lake–of course there was no place to put a sail as large as Rhode Island but in the front hatch and V-berth–not a popular course of action for my wife. It's no wonder that I can't find the spinnaker anymore. Ash tragically died in a car accident in June 2009. Of course, we continue to see Mary every year.

Its hard to sail across the Lake
And not think of you
White capped seas and southwest breeze
Our spinnaker in our wake

A zest for life a lovely wife
Gin and dinner we often shared
Adventure and laughter and the unexpected
With you was daily fare

Open waters and open skies
Was the god you chose to serve
We fished for perch our minds renewed
But couldn't feed the multitudes
But enough for small hors d'ouvres

You taught the rule of Happy Law
Only three weeks vacation was my faux paus
Your retirement was just a kick
With stocks and wood and funny stones
Your days were full and your light full shone
Old dogs can truly learn new tricks

Through memories I search and sift
To understand your greatest gift
The one through life that we will hold and carry
But of course, the friend you left in Mary

For Doug and Diane

Another great friend is Doug Shepard and his wife Diane, also from the Port Dover area. Doug and Diane have a C&C 35 named Passage and continue to sail in Long Point Bay and Lake Erie as they enter their seventies. A retired lawyer, Doug has shown me the workings of the Canadian legal system, and Diane (a retired English teacher) gave me a big boost of confidence to compile and publish my poetry. Whenever I find a bottle of red wine, usually Argentine, at my dock, I know that Doug is nearby.

Old friends at a dock in Erie
A little more gray and a few more wrinkles
Calmly they throw us their lines as they dock in Erie
And we are together again.

After dinner the wine poured freely
Under a sky of stars and stray meteors
The conversation has been forgotten
But not the warmth of the evening
The better the friendship the fewer the words
There is great meaning in friendship

The morning came early
Our coffee was made
As she squinted into the rising sun
And pulled away from the dock
As we gently handed their lines to them

He waved goodbye from the foredeck
And began to collect his tangle of lines
Stepping cautiously amidst the clutter
A fresh breeze and the morning sun lit his face

Red Dog's Lament

Our friend and colleague Art Benson died suddenly in September, 2009. Art and his boat Red Dog were inseparable, both in real life and legend, from the Lake Erie Islands to Buffalo.

She knew that something wasn't right
when he didn't return that Friday night
She listened quietly to the tick of the clock
and sat there all night by the side of the dock

Some say she was nothing more than an inanimate mass
six tons of aluminum, teak and old fiberglass
Of course her decks were scuffed and the luster was gone
but she knew about love and knew how to respond

For 23 years through storms she had carried him
and the wonderful woman who had just married him
He kept her well scrubbed and her teak clean and bright
never carried much gas but the fridge bulged with Bud light

With Art at the wheel adventure took wing
He made her feel special, a real living thing
Crashing through waves, water over the rail
Starry skies and fried chicken and late night tales,
no matter how often he told them, they never grew stale

He took her to Scudder and the Bay and Port Stanley
She soon was the center of his family
He took her to beaches and ports all around
never led her astray but sometimes aground
Often at the dock she waited patiently with Bonnie
for Art to find home with Jim, Sam or Ronnie

She's old enough to know the end of a fling
but knows that winter is followed always by spring
She knows there will be more days of breezy beam reaching
but looks past her windex to the night stars, beseeching
the wind gods, with whom her rigging once sang
to transform her, once more, into a real living thing

We shall continue to sail and answer the midnight call
of the offshore breeze and the *Red Dog* that lies within us all

Weathering Storms

With a little help from Peter, Paul and Mary

At times like this it's hard to state
the words to comfort, the pain to abate
Our darkest thoughts are churned over and over again
tormenting our most inner soul with what could have been.

But the fact remains we just don't know
when and where the gale winds blow
But, without hesitation, we still set sail
for the open lake to return or fail

We can beat into the wind with waves ten feet high
or jibe around and fly the spinnaker with pole set high
to ride the waves and breeze to an unseen shore
knowing after every storm there's always one more.

It's a new day and the night's storms past
Friends will help haul your main up your broken mast
Your sails may back and stall, but you will find your breeze
Ride the reach, and let your mind and jibsheets ease

Sometimes it takes a lot of tacks to find our way home
While you're out there tacking around just don't tack alone
Keep your face to the wind

Adieu

*My mother lived in Las Vegas until her death
in 1997. She loved to visit northeastern Ohio
and loved the lush green summer months.
Most of all, she loved to sail on Lake Erie, and
she made her last wishes known.*

White capped waves splashed and glistened in the afternoon sun
boldly the breeze across a blue sky blew where clouds were none
seven vessels with white wings like angels flew
north to open seas to gather once more to honor you
and to find your particular place and bid you adieu.

We found your place in open seas as the sun hung low
where the water runs deep and the warm winds blow
where the wind and water become almost as one
a quiet place for you after your race was won

Your friends and your family were there at the appointed hour
to offer a silent prayer and drop a yellow flower
our fingers ached as we touched you once again
as we dipped into the box and brought you home to waves and wind.

Connections

I have written this poetry over the course of twenty years without a thought toward some day collecting them in a book. Each poem was written after particular events, or during particular moods, and expresses a thought or maybe an observation. Each poem was always meant to stand on its own and was never intended to be part of something larger or to attain a higher meaning. And, yet, each poem is part of the whole and, like so much else in life, perhaps the whole is greater than the sum of its parts. Each poem can be a dot and can stand alone or, on our whim, be connected into something larger than the poem itself.

In the end, I suppose, whether to stand alone or be part of something larger may be a choice we all make. But, such a choice may be somewhat illusory: for we are individuals and free to follow our dreams, and yet we are clearly part of something much larger than ourselves. The 17th century poet and philosopher John Donne understood this when he famously wrote:

> No man is an island
> Entire of itself
> Each is a piece of the continent
> A part of the main
> If a clod is washed to the sea
> Europe is less
> As well as if a promontory were
> As well as if a manor of thine own
> Or of thine friends were
> Each man's death diminishes me
> For I am involved with mankind
> Therefore send not to know
> For whom the bell tolls
> It tolls for thee.

But the connections run much deeper than John Donne imagined. The 18th century poet Samuel Taylor Coleridge reached this conclusion in his epic poem the Rime of the Ancient Mariner, about an old sailor who kills an albatross for no reason and suffers grievous consequences for his deed. At the end of the poem, he is explaining to another guest at a wedding the lessons he has learned: namely, that all life is connected and is to be cherished.

> Farewell, farewell for this I tell
> To thee thou wedding guest
> He prayeth well who loveth well
> Both Man and bird and beast
> He prayeth best who loveth best
> All things great and small
> For the dear God who loveth us
> He made and loveth all.

And yet, the connections run still deeper and more powerful. Those of us who sail upon the Lake, or fish in streams and rivers or climb mountains become intimate with the Lake, or stream or mountain. We become one with our surroundings.

The Lake has become an important part of my life, much more than just drinking its water. I see the Lake almost daily—it is the most significant geological feature for hundreds of miles. When sailing upon her waters, I acknowledge that I am sailing on a Lake created by glaciers a mile thick and more than 10,000 years ago during the Last Ice Age, and long before the Pyramids or even recorded human history.

There is more to the Connection, because Lake Erie does not stand by itself; rather the Lake is part of a massive fresh water system we call the Great Lakes, and the Lake is fed by water running from those Lakes. These Lakes, in turn, are fed by rainfall collected in a giant basin in the upper Midwest and Canada. The rainfall, in turn, is connected to moisture brought by the prevailing winds from the Pacific and its interaction with competing warm and cold fronts from the Gulf of Mexico and the Arctic Circle. And of course, moisture and fronts depend on the sun.

Sailing on the Lake brings the Connection up front and personal. I like the breezy days when the waves are high and the boat plunges up and down waves, spraying water over the bow and often into the cockpit soaking all concerned (of course this is better on hot summer days as opposed to the first week of May when the water temperature may be in the low to mid 40's). What is interesting, however, is that such conditions easily blur distinctions between the Lake, the breeze, the sun and ourselves. At such times we are reminded, sometimes in a cold and uncomfortable way, that we are intimately connected with all that surrounds us.

It should be no surprise that the Connection extends to the boat, which is the only thing separating us on the Lake from serious danger. Every sailor I know has encountered Lake conditions which scared them; it's part of Life, we all learn to deal with it and we learn to embellish the stories whenever we gather for a drink. Importantly, every sailor walks away from those experiences with a new found appreciation, if not love, for their boat. We maintain and clean our boats, and we learn these boats can take more bad weather than we can. Consequently, we learn that if we are caught in a bad storm on the Lake, stay away from the shoreline, rocks and shallow water. The boat will protect us.

It is no wonder that sailors from the beginning of time have given names to their boats and treat them as a family member. Boat names are always chosen with care; you never see boats named "Slug" or "Death Trap", even when an objective viewpoint would conclude that such a boat would be aptly named. Rather, boats are named after lovers, mothers or virtues we hold dear because the boat is part of us and we of her.

I have digressed and almost forgot the point I wanted to make, always indicative of both aging and a reminder that it's time to bring this book to a close.

So, let me close. The connection between each individual poem in this book is in fact the Connection. The poetry, collectively and better than any individual poem can express, acknowledges and celebrates the ways we are connected to each other, to the Life that surrounds us, the Lake and even the "inanimate" fiberglass boats that jump alive whenever we venture beyond the breakwall.

Be Curious. L'Chaim!

AUTHOR'S NOTE

Kyle B. Smith is a practicing attorney in Ashtabula County, Ohio with the firm of Smith and Miller in Jefferson, Ohio. He was raised in Orange County, California, and raised steers and oranges as part of his 4-H work. He graduated with a BA in history from the University of California, Davis and a J.D. from Willamette University in Salem, Oregon. He left the West Coast in 1980 to teach at the University of Toledo Law School and worked his way to Ashtabula County in 1982 where he first worked with Ashtabula County Legal Aid. He has served as the Assistant Solicitor in Ashtabula, Ohio and the Law Director in Conneaut, Ohio. He currently serves as Solicitor for the Villages of Roaming Shores and Geneva on the Lake. Kyle lives with his wife Lorraine in Conneaut and a handful of cats, where he enjoys fiddling, writing and woodworking in his spare time.

Photography by Terry Persily, Gary Fritts, Don Stark, Mike Adlay, Brad Arnold. and Joe Scott

Design by Steven Gibbens

Typeface-Avenir Next (9/12), Eastwood (23/22)

Made in United States
Orlando, FL
15 December 2024